ear Mrs. K:

this is for you. I've had it for a been comforting to skim through when I need an extra boost. I haven't looked through it as often as I should Anyway, when I saw the title I felt that it should be yours (I think God told me so.) and I hope it brings you a ton of comfort and reminders of who is the <u>biggest</u> one of all!)

Hi... I'm back:) I was just thinking some more... you've helped with so much! I can never forget the Phillipians verse can do all things through Christ who strengthens me" love Him so much... I wonder how many other lives you've nowingly touched because of that love get scared and doubt a lot so I just wanted to share e comforts that have helped me: when you take communion think of Jesus as the bread en you chew it that He's going straight to your heart you think of the whole "feed on Him with/in your hearts by h with Thanksgiving" you can "eat" Jesus (the word all day ๑ all night)

→

- imagining that whenever your scared that Jesus is a Prince at a ball asking you to come dance with him (if it's really hard to believe it then imagine He's letting you stand on top of his feet while he dances/leads)

- simply praising (remembering all the great things/blessings God has given) it's hard if you don't feel like it but when you remember the good stuff it helps.

here's a verse from a Spanish poet:

"You, like the night, to sweet repose invite us upon the pillow of your pallid, naked and quiet breast... There to rest you invite our sunken foreheads bent by the weight of our storm-clouded sorrows... And our deep sorrows rest on your heart, the unexhausted fountain of eternal humanity and there, as in ocean on which the changeless quiet of heaven is mirrored, they fall asleep, and dream"
Miguel de Unamuno

"If we genuinely love people, we desire for them far more than it is within our power to give, and that will cause us to pray..." (not sure who said this)

one more... just remember God never gives up on us
I love you! (and of course so does He!)

I'm Ready for My Rainbow, Lord

I'M READY FOR MY RAINBOW, LORD

JOY MORGAN DAVIS

Fleming H. Revell
A Division of Baker Book House
Grand Rapids, Michigan 49516

©1998 by Joy Morgan Davis

Published by Fleming H. Revell
a division of Baker Book House Company
P.O. Box 6287, Grand Rapids, MI 49516-6287

Printed in the United States of America

Library of Congress Cataloging-in-Publication Data

Davis, Joy Morgan.
    I'm ready for my rainbow, Lord / Joy Morgan Davis.
        p.   cm.
    ISBN 0-8007-7167-2 (hardcover)
    1. Christian poetry, American. I. Title.
    PS3554.A9349126I18   1998
    811'.54—dc21   98-5013

For information about all new releases from Baker Book House, visit our web site:
http://www.bakerbooks.com

CONTENTS

Contents

Faith: Mountains and Mustard Seeds

Rainbows: Umbrellas of Belief

WHAT NOAH SAW

Today, Lord,
I so desperately need
For You to give *me*
All that You gave
Noah . . .
Faith, to follow a course
I cannot comprehend.
Wisdom, to build
A worthy ark.
Peace, when the
Rains fall and the
Floodwaters rise . . .
And finally,
Your precious
Promise!

O Lord,
I so need to see
What Noah saw . . .

I'm so ready for
My rainbow!

PATIENCE:
WAITING FOR SOON

WAITING FOR SOON

It seems I'm
Always waiting for
Soon, Lord!

How often I've
Thought: It will
Surely happen soon . . .
Or, This will be
Over soon . . .
Or, SOON things will be
Just as I've
Always wanted!

If SOON
Is coming, Lord,
When will it be . . .
It seems so late
Already!

O Child,
When is not
Important here . . .
(Soon may be tomorrow,
Or it may not be
Until eternity)!
Meanwhile *waiting*
Is important . . .
For patience is
The evidence of hope,
And hope is
The evidence of faith,
And faith is the
Evidence of
Things unseen . . .

Including the "soon"
You so desire!

TELL ME THE TIME

What time *is* it,
Lord?!
I know Your Word says
There's a time for
Everything
Under the sun . . .
A time to be born, a time
To die,
A time to sow, a time
To reap,
A time to laugh, a time
To cry . . .
But often I'm not sure
WHICH
I should do
WHEN!

Should I stand stoic,
Enduring the status quo,
Or should I try to move
Heaven and earth to
Change things?!
Should I speak my mind
Or hold my tongue?!
Should I march righteously
Into the Red Sea,

Or should I use the good sense
You gave me and stay high,
Dry, sensible, and safe?!

It's such a dilemma,
Lord!
I'm listening . . .
Just tell me the time!

Beginning of Time

Sometimes, Lord,
There's a tomorrow
That promises to be
So exciting
I wake up in the
Middle of the night
Wishing it was
Morning!

I just want it
To BEGIN . . .
I want it
To be time!

I wonder . . .
Is this how You felt
Just before the
Dawn of Creation?

FLAME OF FAITH

Lord, I've long prayed for
Light on this subject . . .
For a sense of
Understanding in
This situation that
So often makes me sad,
For Your clear
Illumination . . .
And finally I've seen
A glimmer!
Not a bright light yet,
But a glimmer!
Like the old oil lamps
That burned low when
First lit,
It's glowing, Lord . . .

Just give me the faith
To fan this little
Flame!

HABAKKUK'S SONG

The prophet
Sang a solemn hymn
To the God
Of his salvation . . .

"Tho' the fig tree
May not blossom
Nor the fruit
Be on the vine . . .
Tho' the fields
Yet yield no food
Nor the flock be
In the fold . . .
Still I will rejoice
In the Lord,
I will joy in
My God!"

Oh, I need music lessons
From Habakkuk,
Lord . . .
I need to know how
To sing when
The drought has
Dried my green pastures,
And wasted away my
Still waters!

IN HIS TIME

Lord, I am so
Impatient to see the
Fruits of my labor!

I know the harvest
Will be bountiful . . .
And I wish I wouldn't
Fidget while it unfolds
One day at a time . . .
But I tend to want it
All at once!

Help me to savor each
Change of seasons.
Make me patient
As I watch and wait through
The rains, the winds,
The dormant days
Of winter.
Give me the peace
Of Your promises.
And then, when finally
The fields are full,
Lead me at last
To the fruit . . .

In Your time.

Casting All Care

It happened, Lord,
As her heart began to break . . .
She turned away,
Holding her hands across
Her breast as if
To hide the breaking
So I couldn't see . . .
But I could hear the sound,
Like ice floes cracking
On a northern lake,
Crushing the leftover limbs
Of fallen trees . . .
Oh, I could hear!

And then like one besieged
She built a sudden shield . . .
Halting those who
Would have followed her
As she retreated toward a
Solitude of time and distance
From her too tender pain,
Too tender to be touched . . .
And finally, now,
She's gone so far that
I can't see or hear or find
Or comfort her!

But I remember, Lord,
The many times *You* left
The multitudes
For lonely hills and valleys
And silent, secret deserts
Where only You
Could find the way . . .
For as You went sorrowing,
Acquainted well with grief,
The deserts became home . . .
Your hiding place.

So as she flees alone
Into that wider
Wilderness
I think You'll surely
Meet her there . . .
And walk and weep a while
With her . . .
And talk until the pain
Becomes more bearable
Because You've borne
It too.

And I will wait,
Still wishing I could
Comfort her . . .
But I'll not worry,
Lord . . .

Assuming she's with You!

Where Have You Been?

I've been busy, Lord,
And we've talked
So briefly
Lately!
I feel flat . . .
Tho' surrounded by
My friends and family
I feel lonesome . . .
Separated from my
Source!
You must have
Missed me too . . .
For I've felt You
Waiting for me . . .
Waiting for me to take
Time for You,
Waiting to fill my
Lonesome soul,

Waiting to restore
The strength,
The peace, the purpose,
The joy of my
Salvation!
Thank You for waiting,
Lord . . .

I'm so sorry I'm late!

GARDENING TOGETHER

I haven't waited for
The world to bring me
Flowers, Lord . . .
I've planted a
Garden!

Now I'm trusting You
To send the rain
For my seeds . . .
And in due season,
The sunshine!

SPEED LIMITS

Dear Lord!
How can I have
So much fulfillment
And still want more?
How can I wish for
Tomorrow before
Today is finished?
Why do I always read
The last chapter
First?
I'm certainly not
Unhappy, Lord . . .
Just in a hurry!

So . . .
Help me to remember that
You have a plan,
A timetable,
A schedule made
Just for me!
Let me really know
That *You* know how
And where and when
It will happen!
Give me the grace
To wait with
Composure . . .

And then, Lord,
Lead me along
The scenic route!

Love That Will Not Let Me Go

Lord,
Just *look* at this
Road I'm on . . .
It's really so rough!
My feet stumble on
Loose rocks,
I frequently fall
Into ruts,
And often I'm stuck
In the miry clay!
I'm still trying,
Lord . . .
Still stubbornly
Trudging along . . .
But my will is weak,
And my strength
Wavers!

O Child,
I see the road
I've allowed you
To walk . . .
It's leading you
Straight to Me!
You'll finish the course,
But in *My* strength,
Not yours . . .
For it's not *your*
Stubborn will
That matters . . .

It's Mine!

WINDSONG

I've hung my harp
On the willows,
Lord!
Like the Israelites
Of old, I'm worn
And weeping . . .
There's no more music
In me . . .
I resign from
Singing!

O Child,
I see your sorrow,
But the music is
Not lost!
Just listen . . .
Don't you hear My
Breezes blowing through
The weeping willows
To stroke the strings
Of your harp?
The song is still
There . . .

And I will play it
Until you return!

Two by Two: One Soul to Another

INTERCESSOR

There's someone I love
Who needs You,
Lord.

Somehow they haven't
Reached You,
Somewhere they've lost
The way,
And sometimes they
Seem to think
The journey is just
Not worth it.
They stand confused,
Afraid to take
Another step.
It breaks my heart
To see them standing
Still . . .
As if life had stopped.

Please, Lord,
Could *You*, perhaps,
Come to *them*?

I'm sure they could
Continue on . . .
If You were walking
With them!

Something's Amiss

Tonight, Lord,
We've both been
Misinterpreted,
Misunderstood,
Misguided,
Mistaken . . .

We've missed the mark,
Missed the point,
Missed the love,
Missed the joy,
And sadly, somehow,
We've missed
Each other.

O Lord,
Help us relearn
The words . . .
For surely "to understand"
Would be much easier
Than "to *mis*understand"!

THERE YOU ARE!

Altho' the sounds of music
Are invisible,
The rich vibrations
Reach my ears . . .
Altho' I cannot see the
Restless wind,
I feel it on my face!

And tho' my earthly eyes
Cannot behold Your
Precious Person, Lord,
The breeze of Your breath
Surrounds me . . .

And I know
You are there!

LEND ME YOUR EARS

It's a lost art . . .
Listening!
I've realized that even
When people look
Directly at you,
They're not really
Listening!
They don't really
Want to hear what you
Think about things,
What hurts, what makes
You happy . . .
And they surely don't want
To deal with any depth,
Any sort of emotion
Or sentimentality . . .
They simply
Can't handle
Communication,
One soul to another soul!

How lonely they must be,
How isolated . . .
Living in such
Soundproof silence!

O Lord,
Since I love to talk
I'm glad you
Love to listen!

My Soul Necessity

I feel betrayed when
Friendship fails
Or romance
Remains unmoved . . .
When what I offer
Is not needed,
When so much is given
And so little
Returned . . .
But to stop giving
Would be to die,
To smother most of
What makes me
Me!
I cannot live with
A hollow hole
In place of my heart,
With nothingness . . .

I have to be complete.

I have to love.

BEQUEST

I thought, Lord,
For so many years,
That I could humanly
Lift my loved ones . . .
Lighten their loads,
Solve their unsettled
Situations,
Surround them with all
I imagined would make
Them happy!

Finally I see
That no matter what
The surroundings
On the *outside*,
The spirit, the mind,
The emotions
Are on the *inside*,
Self-contained . . .
And can't be touched
Except by You!

So, Lord,
I will remind You often
Of their names and
Their needs . . .

And then I will
Leave them to Heaven!

RESTORATION

I'm so sad,
Lord . . .
A long relationship
Has tarnished . . .
A sharing friendship
Has become a
Dull indifference!
I've tried to restore
Its luster,
To make it shine
Once more,
But we're so isolated
From each other now,
(And silence is
Not golden)!
What should I do,
Lord . . .
What should
I say?

Patience, Child . . .
Let not your heart
Be troubled.
I know what has
Been lost,
I see there is
No luster!
You pray . . .

And I'll polish!

MEETING PLACE

It hurts so much,
Dear Lord, so much . . .
The angry argument that
Built a barrier so
High and wide and terrible
We can't see or hear
Or touch each other . . .
I want it
Down
Dismantled
Moved
Before it breaks my heart!
Teach us how, Lord . . .
Tell us how!

Dear Children,
When each of you is willing
To accept
The other's pain
And hold it to yourself
As if it were
Your own,
Then the barrier will be
Changed, completely
Rearranged . . .

And the wall becomes
A bridge
On which you meet!

Tell Me, Touch Me

I'm so grateful,
Dear Lord,
For the many manners
Of *expression*
We humans have!
You gave us
Voices to raise
In prayer and praise . . .
You gave us
Poetry, and prose,
And song,
And the sometimes
Silent language
Of love . . .
You gave us hands
And hearts that
Reach out for
Each other!
How barren we
Would be
If we could not
Communicate!

Yes, You made us
Like Yourself . . .
Able to *express*
Emotions . . .
Able to shout for joy
Or sigh in sorrow
Or touch with
Tenderness!

Oh, let us not neglect
So great a gift . . .
Especially with those
We love!

FLOODS:
TEMPORARY TEMPESTS,
LINGERING LOVE

LASTING

A tempest,
No matter how furious,
Is temporary.
It's the long,
Lingering days of
Dull heat or
Constant cold or
Relentless rain that
Can cause a fatal crack
In the foundation . . .
Or my faith.

I'm so glad the Savior
Said, "I am with you always!"

Now I know that
Through the
Heat and cold
And relentless rain
Of life . . .

His love is
Lingering!

THROUGH THE VALLEY

Surely the most
Soul-shattering pain
Of the cross
Was not the flood
Of suffering,
But the final separation
From the Father . . .
"My God," the Savior cried,
"Why hast Thou forsaken Me?"

That is the sacrifice
Which overwhelms
Me most!
He died comfortless
And alone . . .
So when *I* pass
Through the valley of
The shadow of death
I can sing the song
Of David . . .
"I will fear no evil,
For Thou art with me!"

Such awesome
Assurance!
No matter where
Or when . . .

I'll never walk alone!

BOUNDLESS

Near the hour of
Her death,
Amy Carmichael sighed,
"I am at the edge
Of the sea . . .
Oh, to swim out
Into the sunrise!"

For that *is* death,
Isn't it . . .
Dawn,
Sunrise,
The misty morning of
Forever . . .

And I wait impatiently
For that first touch of
Gold upon the sea,
That first light from
The other shore,
That final
Dawning . . .
For then I will
Lay aside life's last
Boundaries . . .

And swim out
To meet the
Sunrise!

HEALED

How would I live,
Lord,
Without refuge?
The battle has left a
Desolate, lonely landscape . . .
And I creep across it,
Wounded and worn,
Into the fortress.

Peace, calm,
Assurance, care . . .
And I am restored to
Stand again.

There truly is
A balm in Gilead.

HARVEST SEASON

Dear Lord,
I've seen that the
Harvest of my hands
Results always
From seeds
That are sown
In my heart . . .

So just now
As my heart is
Being pulled apart
By this new sorrow,
Help me to look upon
These torn furrows
As newly fallowed ground,
Plowed for planting.

Come today, Dear Lord,
While the soil is still
Moist with my tears . . .
Plant Your seeds of
Fruitful faith . . .

And from my
Heart's upheaval
I will present to You
A precious harvest!

LEAST OF ALL

O Lord,
My little pile of ashes,
My simple sorrows
Seem so small
Compared to others
Who suffer
So much more.

But there they are,
Those ashes . . .
Reminding me that
Something in my life . . .
Some dream
Some deep desire
Some precious plan
Is gone,
Disintegrated
Into dust.

So, Lord,
Is Your promise
For me too?
My loss seems small
And my sorrow
Insignificant
But my heart
Still hurts,
And hurts . . .
   And hurts . . .
Will I too, someday,
Receive beauty
For my ashes?

Child of Mine,
You say your loss
Is small . . .
But so is
The sparrow!

THE BUILDER

It has always seemed
A poignant picture
To me, Lord . . .
A weeping Nehemiah
Riding alone in the night
To survey the wreckage
Of Jerusalem's walls.

The vision that night
Was Yours,
But the vow was his . . .
To rebuild according
To Your specific plans!

So, Lord, when *my* walls
Begin to fall . . .
The foundations shaken
By those predators
Of darkness who would
Wreck my fortress
And leave my faith
In ruins . . .
Let me remember
Nehemiah,
Riding alone
On a moonlit night . . .

And I will know
You have the perfect
Specifications
For my new walls!

JUST ENOUGH

I believe, Lord,
That the best blessing
In being Your child
Is that You know
My limitations . . .
You know the length
Of my strength . . .
And whenever You've
Asked me to
Prevail,
You've always promised
Eventual victory!
You've also promised
That one day I shall look
For those who would
Destroy me
And they shall not
Be found!

I look forward to
That day, Lord!

Until then
I assume my resources
Will last . . .
Since You are the one
Who has stocked the
Storehouse of
My life!

Back to the Future

I realize, Lord,
We are on the verge of
The twenty-first century . . .
But must ELECTRONICS
Rule our lives?!
I have friends who
Have formed an attachment
To their computers
Stronger than
Most marriages,
Others who play
Chess and Parcheesi
On synchronized sound waves,

And others who would rather
Roam that vast, invisible
Roadway of information
In the sky
Than take a picnic
To the park!
There is now a new
Generation of children
To whom computers are
No challenge . . .
They compose music, poetry,
Lists, their lives
On compact discs!

Oh, I know it's now
The FUTURE,
And mass communication
Is here to stay . . .
I'm just glad I don't
Have to *fax* my hopes
And dreams and inner needs
To You!
I'm sure a lot would be lost
In the translation . . .

Like my tears, my sighs,
And my songs of joy!

THE PEACEABLE PLACE

I've happened upon
A hidden treasure,
Lord . . .
Your hushed whispers
In my heart!

Congregations can worship
With hosannas,
Crowds can be mesmerized
As a mighty firmament
Roars and flashes,
But Your whispers are
Not heard except
In solitude!

In the silence Your
Wise ways are
Revealed to me . . .
Your direction,
Your rest . . .
Oh, especially Your rest,
For often I cannot face
Another moment of
This NOISE!

I've learned that
I must release the
Clamor of life . . .
The loud call of
Lost causes,
The clanging of
Distant distractions . . .
For only then
Can I hear the promises
That are so personal,
The encouragement that
Is for me alone,
The soul-sounds that
End my questioning
And enable me to reach
This peaceable place.

O Lord,
Keep me quiet . . .

And keep whispering
To my heart!

Firm Footing

Here I am again, Lord . . .
Sinking!

I walk on spiritual waters
For just so long,
And then I look
Around me . . .
The waves are so high,
And I am so heavy . . .
Help me!
Please, help me!

O Child, come closer,
Just come closer . . .
Stay in step
With Me!
There now . . .
Is that better?

Much better, Lord!
My eyes are still wet . . .

But my feet are dry!

FAITH: MOUNTAINS AND MUSTARD SEEDS

MOUNTAINS AND MUSTARD SEEDS

Faith, the size of a
Mustard seed,
Should move mountains
We're told!
So we've looked at
The peaks . . .
Those piles of earth
And rock and stone . . .
And we've thought
Our faith was small
When they stood
Still!

But now I know
God never meant the
Mountains of the
Earth . . .
For these mountains
Can be moved by
Bulldozers and dynamite!

It's the mountains
Of the spirit
That take faith . . .
Mountains of doubt
And disagreement,
Piles of heartache
And hurt,
Peaks that separate
And divide,
These can be flattened
Only by faith . . .
And for these
My mustard seeds
Are multiplied!

I *have* moved
Mountains!

Travel Tips

I've never learned to
Travel light . . .
I have *major*
Baggage!
For a three-day trip
I take six pairs
Of shoes . . .
With matching purses!
I want all my STUFF
Around me . . .
My appliances,
Hot curlers, irons,
My own pillow!
I have made a mockery
Of the man who said
You can't take it
With you . . .
I can!

At least I can
For now.

But what about later?!
What about that last,
Everlasting time
When I go to glory . . .
What can I take then?!

Not money
Nor fame nor fortune . . .
Not my good wishes
Or my good works . . .
I'll leave all those
Behind!
I'll leave behind also
Life's accumulated
"Baggage" . . .
All the burdens,
The sickness, the sorrow,
My sin!

So, unencumbered
I will go,
Freely . . .
With only my FAITH
Enfolding me,
The only garment
I will ever need
To enter glory!
And what a relief
It will be . . .

To travel light
At last!

Who He Is

Dear Lord . . .
If ever I ask "Why?"
Help me to remember
That Your ways
Are not my ways,
That Your thoughts
Are not my thoughts,
And that even as
The heavens are higher
Than the earth
So are Your thoughts,
Your ways, Your wonders
Higher than mine!
Remind me that You
Will always be a
Mystery to me . . .

That all I will ever
Need to know is
That you are God . . .
Omnipotent
   But also tender,
Masterful
   But also merciful,
Sovereign
   But also Savior . . .

For when I know
Who You are,
Then "Why" is
No longer relevant.

SHIELDED

You'd think that
Satan would get tired
Of trying to
Trip me up . . .
He is constantly
Throwing obstacles in
My way . . .
Everything from rocks
To hand grenades!

Sometimes I don't see
Them coming
So I slip and fall . . .
But then the Savior
Reaches down to
Help me . . .
And with that touch,
That contact between
His hand and mine,
I stand up stronger
Than ever!

You'd think Satan would
Get tired of waging
A war he can't win . . .

Doesn't he know
I get up every morning
And put on the
Whole armor of God?!

BIBLE STORY

She packed her son
A lunch . . .
Five loaves
And two fish
Along with her
Love and prayers . . .
And she said, "My son,
Today I want you to
Follow Jesus,
And listen to all
His words!"
And soon her son was
In the middle of
A miracle!

Centuries later
I decided to do the same
For *my* son . . .
Pack his lunch with
Love and prayers and
All the wisdom I could
Gather together . . .
Then send him to
Follow Jesus!

It was the only way
I could be sure
The lunch would last
A lifetime . . .

And just maybe
Be multiplied into
A miracle!

REMEDY

An inquisitive child
Asked, "If I *forget*
A thing, will my head
Be lighter?"

Probably not . . .

But come to think
Of it,
Maybe I *could* take a
Load off my mind
If I forgot
A few things . . .
Grudges,
Resentments,
Insults, injuries!

That would certainly
Clear the way for more
Patience,
  Compassion,
     Pardon . . .

And very possibly
Fewer headaches!

LIGHT IN THE DARK

Lord,
I tossed and turned
And fretted
And plumped my pillows
And *finally*
I got up and opened
Your Word!
And there it was . . .
The answer
The solution
The revelation
I had so anxiously
Wanted!

O Lord,
You never fail to
Say the right thing!
In fact . . .

You never fail!

Someone to Talk To

Last night I had this
Really ridiculous
Dream . . .
I thought I had
Called heaven,
And I heard, "Thank you
For calling . . .
For help, press one!
For assurance, press two!
For guidance, press three!
For answered prayer,
Press four . . .
And if you still need
To talk to Someone,
Stay on the line!"

What a relief, Lord,
To wake up and realize
That I only have to
Call *Your name* . . .

For all of the above!

SIMPLE TO ASSEMBLE

I know, Lord,
You gave me great
Directions . . .
Simple step by step
Instructions
That anyone could
Follow . . .
But somewhere back there
I must have missed
A cue,
Overlooked a line,
Maybe skipped a step
Or two . . .
Because I can't *believe*
The mess I've made!

I've got just one question,
Lord . . .
What is Plan B?!

OLD ENOUGH

They tell me, Lord,
That to be
Truly mature
I must accept defeat
And unfair fate
With the grace of
A woman,
Instead of the
Petulant grief of
A child.

But at this moment,
As I remember
Those lost treasures
Of my heart . . .
The longing that was
Never realized,
The offered gift
That was never opened,
The sacrifice that was
Finally forsaken . . .
I don't feel childish
At all.

I feel old . . .

And wise enough
To know that sometimes
The most mature grace
Is to grieve.

NOT TO WORRY

It began so well,
Lord . . .
When You presented me
With such a proud
Assignment!
It was going to be so
Wonderful and fine
And fortunate!
But then the problems
Began to appear . . .
Confusion,
Frustration,
Unproductive days . . .
I was sweeping leaves
Against the wind,
And I wondered
WHY!

But finally, Lord,
I've felt reassured . . .
For I sense that all
This distraction,
The detours,
The delays,
Have been hastily
Thrown into the way
By Satan,
Desperate to dismantle
Or diminish such a
Superlative plan!

Therefore it has
Occurred to me that
This assignment,
So subtly besieged
And sabotaged,
Must be destined for
Absolutely soaring
Success . . .

Else Satan wouldn't
Be so seriously
At war!

WHAT PRICE VICTORY?

Lord Jesus,
Whenever I wonder
Why the trouble and trial,
I think of the centurion
At the cross . . .
He was converted not
By Your life,
  Or Your love,
    Or Your manifest
Miracles . . .
He was converted by
Your selfless
Suffering.

So, if this sorrow
That now crushes me beneath
An unseen cross
Can cause one soul to
See You
Through me,
Then I will not have
Suffered in vain . . .

But in victory!

RAINBOWS: UMBRELLAS OF BELIEF

WEATHER WATCH

I don't know what
Tomorrow will be,
Lord . . .
But *today* is
Lovely!

I've tried to prepare
For all sorts of
Weather . . .
If it rains I've got
Umbrellas of belief,
If it's dark I've got
Candles of faith,
If it's cold I've got
A cloak of courage!

But today,
Lord,
It's *lovely* . . .
And all I need is
A large capacity to
Rejoice, to be glad . . .

And to properly praise
Your unbelievable
BEING!

Beams from Above

Tonight the shadow
Of the earth
Covered the moon
Causing a
Total eclipse . . .
For a time
We could not see
The silver circle,
Bathe in its beams,
Or follow its
Light.

O Lord,
I'm so glad
There's never an
Eclipse of
Your love . . .

For I depend
Upon it,
Night and day!

NEW YEAR'S EVE

The days ahead seem so
Uncertain!
What will happen to my health,
My love, my relationships,
My work . . .
There's so much to be done,
So little time,
Never enough strength . . .
My enthusiasm is
Fragmented, my energy
Divided,
I feel confused and
Vaguely vulnerable to a
Future that so far holds
Only loose ends . . .
Unsure, unsettled,
Uncertain.

But wait! There is the Word . . .
"He will not allow
Your foot to slip!
He who keeps you will
Neither slumber
Nor sleep!"

Dear God in Heaven,
Of You I am certainly
Certain!

Happy new year.

SPECIFIC

Dear Lord,
I love it when You
Answer me with Your Word,
Like yesterday when I felt
Lost in the crowd of Christians . . .
One among so many millions,
All believing, all belonging,
All under Your watchcare . . .
But I wondered if You ever
Saw *me* in the
Multitude,
If You ever gave *me*
A second thought!

Then I read a psalm . . .
"I am poor and needy,
Yet the Lord *takes thought*,
And *plans* for me!"

O Lord! Not only do You
Think of me . . .
You've made me an
Agenda!

PROMISE

Lord,
It's winter in my life
Just now . . .
Even my tears are frozen
Before they fall
From my face . . .
Do You know?
Do You see?
Do You see me
Shivering
In the cold?

O Child,
I see! I also
Understand . . .
That's why I made
The seasons!
Always after winter
There is spring . . .

Trust Me!

CATHEDRAL

We worshipped today,
Dear Lord,
In one of Your
Holy of holies . . .
Deep within a
Redwood forest!
We walked in wonder
Through the dark
Green grottos
As sunlight sifted down
Like gold dust
Through a thousand
Lacy leaves . . .
(I never knew before
That those towering
Sentinels of the centuries
Produced such delicate
Little leaves . . .
Spread out in sprays
Like layers upon layers
Of feathery fans!)

What a hidden,
Hallowed place it was . . .
Where the only sound
Was silence,
Where words became
A pale expression
Beside the song
Of souls,
Where Your spirit spoke
Through personal
Inspiration . . .

And in such a sacred,
Rare cathedral
How could we not
Bow before
Your majesty!

Awesome

Today I decided
To count my blessings . . .
But I gave up!
It was like standing
In front of a
Christmas tree
Trying to count the
Lights!

O Lord . . .
You do a great job
Of decorating
A life!

THE PERSONAL TOUCH

Lord,
It was the most
Remarkable moment
When I looked at my life
And realized that *You* . . .
Creator of the Universe,
Savior of the World,
Sovereign of all
Time and Eternity . . .
Had reached down and
Touched *me*!
How on earth could You
See *me*, know *me*,
Separate *me* from all the
Millions more who love you?

How could You have
Led my life
In such a personal,
Private, precious way?!
I cannot imagine how,
Lord,
But You have . . .

And I kneel
In awe, wonder,
And worship!

FORECAST

No rain today,
Lord!

It was predicted . . .
We expected it
Prepared for it
Waited for it
But the skies are blue
And the clouds are
Fine and fluffy!
What a relief . . .
No rain!

I've noticed that You
Do this now and then
In my life, Lord . . .
Send blue skies
When I've expected
Rough weather . . .
For my own predictions
Are so often wrong
As I waste time
With storm windows
And worry
When I should be
Resting in You!

Since it's my future
That's affected by
The forecast,
I'm so glad one of us
Is weather-wise!

CURTAIN CALL

In this world
We always want a
Happy ending . . .
We want dreams come true
And hopes fulfilled!

But in reality,
We will wake from
The dream.
We will realize that
Happiness is not
For "all time"
And we will settle
For "sometime."
As for hope,
We will learn that it
Always assumes a
Self-sacrifice,
As we give ourselves
To bring about the
Things for which
We have hoped.

Life can be
Beautiful . . .
But it is never,
Ever easy!
How I look forward
To God's FOREVER AFTER . . .

Now that's what I call
A Happy Ending!